CW01630681

Oscar Wilde in quote

ISBN: 1 86476 119 9

Copyright © Axiom Publishing, 2001.
Unit 2, 1 Union Street, Stepney, South Australia, 5069.
This book is copyright. Apart from any fair dealing for the purpose of private study, research, criticism or review, as permitted under the Copyright Act, no part may be reproduced by any process without written permission. Enquiries should be made to the publisher.

This edition for
SELECT EDITIONS
Devizes
Wiltshire, UK

Oscar Wilde

in quote

ADVICE

I always pass on good advice.
It is the only thing to do with it.
It is never any use to oneself.

It is always a silly thing to give advice,
but to give good advice is absolutely fatal.

AGE

I have never admitted that I am more
than twenty-nine, or thirty at the most.
Twenty-nine when there are pink shades,
thirty when there are not.

Thirty-five is a very attractive age,
London society is full of women
of the highest birth who have,
of their own free choice,
remained thirty-five for years.

As for the aged,
I always contradict the aged.
I do it on principle.
If you ask them their opinion on
something that happened yesterday,
they solemnly give you
the opinions current in 1820,
when people wore high stocks,
believed in everything, and
knew absolutely nothing.

AMERICA

Everybody (in America)
seems in a hurry to catch a train.
This is a state of things which is
not favourable to poetry or romance.

In America, the young are always
ready to give those who are older
than themselves the full benefit
of their inexperience.

It is a vulgar error to suppose that
America was ever discovered.
It was merely detected.

Marriage is hardly a thing one can do
now and then—except in America.

APPEARANCES

Both Irving's legs are delicately intellectual, but his left leg is a poem.

He had the sort of face that, once seen, is never remembered.

To be natural is such a very difficult pose to keep up.

To me beauty is the wonder of wonders. It is only the shallow people who do not judge by appearance.
The true mystery of the world is the visible not the invisible

ART

Art is the only serious thing in the world.
And the artist is the only person
who is never serious.

Art never expresses anything but itself.

Bad artist always admire each other's work.

It is only an auctioneer who can equally
and impartially admire all schools of art.

Most of our modern portrait painters are
doomed to absolute oblivion.
They never paint what they see.
They paint what the public sees,
and the public never sees anything.

Vice and virtue are to the artist
materials for an art.

Beauty

At least
I have not made my heart
a heart of stone,
Nor starved my boyhood
of its goodly feast,
Nor walked where Beauty
is a thing unknown.

Those who find beautiful meanings in beautiful things are the cultivated. For these there is hope.

It is better to be beautiful
than to be good, but it is better to be good than to be ugly.

Body & Soul

Nothing can cure the soul but the senses,
just as nothing can cure the senses
but the soul.

The harmony of soul and body—
how much that is!
We in our madness have separated
the two, and have invented a realism
that is vulgar, an ideality that is void.

The soul is born old, but grows young.
That is the comedy of life.
The body is born young and grows old.
That is life's tragedy.

Those who see any difference between
soul and body have neither.

Cleverness

"I like hearing myself talk.
It is one of my greatest pleasures.
I often have long conversations
all by myself, and I am so clever that
sometimes I don't understand a single
word of what I am saying."

JACK: I am sick to death of cleverness. Everybody is clever nowadays. You can't go anywhere without meeting clever people. The thing has become an absolute public nuisance.
I wish to goodness we had a few fools left.
ALGERNON: We have.
JACK: I should extremely like to meet them. What do they talk about?
ALGERNON: The fools? Oh! about clever people of course.
JACK: What fools.

CLOTHES

A really well-made buttonhole is the only link between Art and Nature.

A well-tied tie
is the first serious step in life.

She wore far too much rouge last night
and not quite enough clothes.
That is always a sign of despair
in a woman.

To Mrs Leverson,
on his release from prison:
My dear, you're the only woman in the world who'd have known the right hat to wear on an occasion like this.

Communication

Talk to every woman as if you loved her,
and to every man as if he bored you,
and at the end of your first season
you will have the reputation of
possessing the most perfect social tact.

There is only one thing in the world
worse than being talked about,
and that is not being talked about.

Whenever one has anything unpleasant
to say, one should always be
quite candid.

CRIME

No crime is valugar, but vulgarity is crime.

Vulgarity is the conduct of others

Nobody ever commits a crime without doing something stupid.

Starvation, and not sin, is parent of modern crime.

The only really humanising influence in prison is the influence of the prisoners.

DEATH

Man is made for something better than disturbing dirt.

No man dies for what he knows to be true. Men die for what they want to be true, for what some terror in their hearts tells them is not true.

Tread light, she is near
Under the snow,
Speak gently, she can hear
The daisies grow.

Requiescat

DEFINITION

Caution:
what we call cowardice in others.

Intuition:
the strange instinct that tell a woman
she is right, whether she is or not.

Pessimist:
one who, when he has the choice
of two evils, chooses both.

Suicide:
the greatest compliment
that one can pay to society.

Dull

Only dull people are brilliant at breakfast.

Only people who look dull
get into the House of Commons,
and only people who are dull
ever succeed there.

We are born in an age when only
the dull are taken seriously, and
I live in terror of not being understood.

Dullness is the coming of age
of seriousness.

DUTY

One's duty as a gentleman should never
interfere with one's pleasure
in the slightest degree.

People are afraid of themselves nowadays.
They have forgotten
the highest of all duties,
he duty that one owes to one's self.

The only duty we owe to history
is to rewrite it.

Woman's first duty in life
is to her dressmaker.
What the second duty is
no one has yet discovered.

English

The English are always
degrading truths into facts.
When a truth becomes a fact
it loses all its intellectual veil.

The English country gentleman
galloping after a fox—
the unspeakable in pursuit
of the uneatable.

The English have a miraculous
power of turning wine into water.

The English public takes
no interest in a work of art
until it is told the work
in question is immoral.

EPIGRAM

An unbiased opinion is always
absolutely worthless.

If one tells the truth, one is sure,
sooner or later, to be found out.

It is difficult not to be unjust
to what one loves.

My own business always bores me
to death; I prefer other people's.

Nothing is so aggravating as calmness.

One can always be kind to people
about whom one cares nothing.

The world is a stage, but the play is badly cast.

FASHION

Fashion is a form of ugliness
so intolerable that we have to alter it
every six months.

Fashion is that by which
the fantastic becomes for the moment
universal.

Fashion is what one wears oneself:
what is unfashionable is what
other people wear.

Food & Drink

I have made an important discovery
...that alcohol, taken in sufficient
quantities, produces all the effects
of intoxication.

Missionaries, my dear!
Don't you realise that missionaries are the divinely provided food for destitute and under-fed cannibals?
Whenever they are on the brink of starvation, Heaven in its infinite mercy sends them a nice plump missionary.

When I am in trouble, eating is the only thing that consoles me.
Indeed, when I am in really great trouble, as anyone who knows me intimately will tell you, I refuse everything except food and drink.

Friendship

An acquaintance that begins with
a compliment is sure to develop
into a real friendship.

Anybody can sympathise with
the suffering of a friend,
but it requires a very fine nature
to sympathise with a friend's success.

Friendship is far more tragic than love.
It lasts longer.

Laughter is not a bad beginning
for a friendship, and it is the best ending
for one.

GOAL

I know not whether Laws be right,
Or whether Laws be wrong;
All that we know who lie in goal
Is that the wall is strong;
And that each day is like a year,
A year whose days are long.
The Ballad of Reading Goal

If this is the way Queen Victoria
treats her prisoners,
she doesn't deserve to have any.
(*On having to wait in the rain for
transportation to take him to prison.*)

Good

It is always with the best intentions
that the worst work is done.

Nowadays so many conceited people
go about Society pretending to be good,
that I think it shows rather a sweet and
modest disposition to pretend to be bad.

There is a great deal of good in
Lord Augustus.
Fortunately it is all on the surface.

You can't make people good by an
Act of Parliament — that's something.

Government

The Lords Temporal say nothing,
the Lords Spiritual have nothing to say,
and the House of Commons
has nothing to say and says it.

There is hardly a single person
in the House of Commons
worth painting, though many of them
would be the better for a little
whitewashing.

Those who try to lead the people
can only do so by following the mob.

HAPPINESS

Some cause happiness wherever they go;
others whenever they go.

The good end happily,
the bad unhappily—
that is what fiction means.

The happiness of a married man
depends on the people he has not
married.

Human Nature

The only thing that one really knows about human nature is that it changes.

The reason we are so pleased to find out other people's secrets is that it distracts public attention from our own.

The true perfection of man
lies not in what man has,
but in what man is.

Whenever a man does a thoroughly stupid thing, it is always from the noblest of motives.

Ideas

An idea that is not dangerous
is unworthy of being called an idea at all.

The value of an idea has nothing
whatsoever to do with the sincerity
of the man who expresses it.
Indeed, the probabilities are that
the more insincere the man is, the more
purely intellectual will the idea be,
as in that case it will not be coloured by
either his wants, his desires,
or his prejudices.

Knowledge

As soon as people are
old enough to know better,
they don't know anything at all.

I must confess that most modern
mysticism seems to me to be simply a
method of imparting useless knowledge
in a form that no one can understand.

The public have an insatiable curiosity
to know everything, except
what is worth knowing.

They show a want of knowledge that
must be the result of years of study.

LAST REFUGE

Ambition is the last refuge of the failure.

Consistency is the last refuge of
the unimaginative.

I adore simple pleasures,
they are the last refuge of the complex.

Seriousness is the only refuge
of the shallow.

Work is the refuge of people who have
nothing better to do.

LIFE

Don't tell me that you have exhausted Life. When a man says that, one knows that Life has exhausted him.

Life is a dream that prevents one from sleeping.

Life is not complex. We are complex. Life is simple and the simple thing is the right thing.

Live! Live the wonderful life
that is in you!
Let nothing be lost upon you.
Be always searching for new sensations.
Be afraid of nothing.

One's real life is so often the life that one does not lead.

LITERATURE

Everyone should keep
someone else's diary.

I am never disappointed in literary men.
I think they are perfectly charming.
It is their works that I find so
disappointing.

I never travel without my diary.
One should always have something
sensational to read in the train.

In old days books where written by men
of letters and read by the public.
Nowadays books are written by the public
and read by nobody.

LITERATURE

One should not be too severe on English novels; they are the only relaxation of the intellectually unemployed.

One would have a heart of stone
to read the death of Little Nell
without laughing.

There is no such thing as a moral or an immoral book. Books are well written, or badly written. That is all.

Marriage

Bigamy is having one wife too many.
Monogamy is the same.

English women conceal their feelings till after they are married.

How marriage ruins a man.
It's as demoralising as cigarettes, and far more expensive.

I was in hopes Lord Illingworth would have married Lady Kelso.
But I believe he said her family was too large. Or was it her feet?

The one charm of marriage is that it makes a life of deception absolutely necessary for both parties.

Men & Women

A woman who can keep a man's love, and love him in return, has done all the world wants of women, or should want of them.

All men are married women's property; that is the only true definition of what married women's property really is.

All women become like their mothers. That is their tragedy. No man does. That's his.

Men always want to be a woman's first love—women like to be a man's last romance.

Men marry because they are tired; women because they are curious. Both are disappointed.

Men & Women

No man has any real success in this world unless he has got woman to back him, and women rule society.

One can always recognise women who trust their husbands, they look so thoroughly unhappy.

The only way a woman can ever reform a man is by boring him so completely that he loses all possible interest in life.

Women are never disarmed by compliments. Men always are. That is the difference between the sexes.

MIND

It has been said that the great events of the world take place in the brain. It is in the brain, and the brain only, that the great sins of the world take place also.

It is not selfish to think for oneself. A man who does not think for himself does not think at all.

The mind of a thoroughly well-informed man is a dreadful thing. It is like a bric-à-brac shop, all monsters and dust, with everything priced above its proper value.

Women represent the triumph of matter over mind, just as men represent the triumph of mind over morals.

MISFORTUNE

Misfortunes one can endure, they come from the outside; but to suffer for one's faults—ah! there is the sting of life.

To have been well brought up
is a great drawback nowadays.
It shuts one out from so much.

To lose one parent, Mr Worthing,
may be regarded as a misfortune;
to lose both looks like carelessness.

MONEY

I don't want money. It is only people who pay their bills who want that, and I never pay mine.

Never buy a thing you don't want merely because it is dear.

No man is rich enough to buy back his past.

One must have some occupation nowadays.
If I hadn't my debts I shouldn't have anything to think about.

Someone's mother lives at Canterbury, where she does a lot of good among the rich.

MORALITY

Morality is simply the attitude we adopt towards people whom we personally dislike.

On an occasion of this kind it becomes more than a moral duty to speak one's mind. It becomes a pleasure.

Scandal is gossip made tedious by morality.

The books that the world calls immoral are books that show the world its own shame.

Music

I assure you that the typewriting machine, when played with expression, is not more annoying that the piano when played by a sister or near relation.

I don't play accurately
—anyone can play accurately
— but I play with wonderful expression.
As far as the piano is concerned,
sentiment is my forte.
I keep science for Life.

If one hears bad music it is one's duty
to drown it in conversation.

Please do not shoot the pianist.
He is doing his best.

People

He knew the precise psychological moment when to say nothing.

Most people are other people. Their thoughts are someone else's opinions, their lives a mimicry, their passions a quotation.

Other people are quite dreadful. The only possible society is one's self.

Zola...is determined to show that, if he has not got genius, he can at least be dull. And how well he succeeds!

PLEASURE

A new Hedonism—
that is what our century needs.

I don't regret for a single moment having lived for pleasure. I did it to the full, as one should do anything that one does ... I lived on honeycomb.

Pleasure is the only thing to live for. Nothing ages like happiness.

Tea is the only pleasure left to us.

POETRY

A poet can survive everything but a misprint.

Inferior poets are absolutely fascinating. The worse their rhymes are, the more picturesque they look. The mere fact of having published a book of second-rate sonnets makes a man quite irresistible. He lives the poetry he cannot write. The others write the poetry that they dare not realise.

There are two ways of disliking poetry, one way is to dislike it, the other is to read Pope.

Poor

I should fancy that the real tragedy of the poor is that they can afford nothing but self-denial.

Really, if the lower orders don't set us a good example, what on earth is the use of them? They seem, as a class, to have absolutely no use of moral responsibility.

To a beggar:
You wretched man, why do you beg when pity is dead?

To recommend thrift to the poor is both grotesque and insulting. It is like advising a man who is starving to eat less.

We are all in the gutter,
but some of us are looking at the stars.

PRINCIPLES

His principles were out of date,
but there was a good deal to be said
for his prejudices.

I like persons better than principles
and I like persons with no principles
better than anything else in the world.

It is personalities not principles
that move the age.

Public

England has done one thing;
it has invented and established public opinion, which is an attempt to organise the ignorance of the community, and to elevate it to the dignity of physical force.

I have no knowledge
of the views of ordinary individuals.

Public opinion exists only
where there are no ideas.

The public is wonderfully tolerant.
It forgives everything except genius.

Relations

I can't help detesting my relations. I suppose it comes from the fact that none of us can stand other people having the same faults as ourselves.

I have invented an invaluable permanent invalid called Bunbury, in order that I may be able to go down into the country whenever I choose.

The longer I live the more keenly I feel that whatever was good enough for our fathers is not good enough for us.

After a good dinner,
one can forgive anybody,
even one's own relatives.

Religion

Ordinary theology has long since converted its gold into lead, and words and phrases that once touched the heart of the world have become wearisome and meaningless through repetition.
If theology desires to move us, she must re-write her formulas.

People fashion their God after their own understanding. They make their God first and worship him afterwards.

Prayer must never be answered: if it is, it ceases to be prayer and becomes correspondence.

Resolutions

Good resolutions are a useless attempt to interfere with scientific laws; their origin pure vanity, their results absolutely nil.

Good resolutions are simply cheques that men draw on a bank where they have no account.

The fatality of good resolutions is that they are always too late.

ROMANCE

One should always be in love.
That is the reason
one should never marry.

The very essence of romance is
uncertainty. If I ever got married,
I'll certainly try to forget the fact.

There is always something ridiculous
about the emotions of people whom one
has ceased to love.

To love oneself is the beginning
of a life-long romance.

SELF-REALISATION

I am far more of an individualist than ever I was. Nothing seems to me of the smallest value except what one gets out of oneself. My nature is seeking a fresh mode of self-realisation.

I am the only person in the world
I should like to know thoroughly,
but I don't see any chance of it
just at present.

We teach people how to remember,
we never teach them how to grow.

Whenever people agree with me.
I always feel I must be wrong.

Shallow People

The people who love only once in their
lives are really the shallow people.
What they call their loyalty and fidelity,
I call either the lethargy of custom or
their lack of imagination.

To me beauty is the wonder of wonders.
It is only the shallow people who do not
judge by appearance.
The true mystery of the world is
the visible, not the invisible.

SIN

Beautiful sins, like beautiful things,
are the privilege of the rich.

Humanity takes itself too seriously.
It is the world's original sin.
If the cavemen had known how to laugh
history would have been different.

Nothing makes one so vain as being told
that one is a sinner.
Conscience makes egotist of all of us.

There is no sin except stupidity.

Stage

I love acting.
It is so much more real than life.

If you hear anything nice said
about the play (*Lady Windermere's Fan*),
write it to me: if not, invent it.

The play was a great success,
but the audience was a disaster.

Women never know when the curtain has fallen. They always want a sixth act, and as soon as the interest of the play is entirely over they propose to continue it.

TEMPTATIONS

I couldn't help it.
I can resist everything except temptation.

The only way to get rid of temptation is to yield to it. Resist it, and your soul grows sick with longing for the things it has forbidden to itself.

There are terrible temptations that it requires strength, strength and courage to yield to.

He is always late on principle,
his principle being that punctuality is the thief of time.

Time is a waste of money.

Truth

If a man is sufficiently unimaginative to produce evidence in support of a lie, he might just as well speak the truth at once.

It is perfectly monstrous the way people go about, nowadays, saying things against one behind one's back that are absolutely and entirely true.

Man is least himself when he talks in his own person. Give him a mask, and he will tell you the truth.

VIRTUE

Don't be misled into the path of virtue.

Each class preaches the importance of those virtues it need not exercise. The rich harp on the value of thrift, the idle grow eloquent over the dignity of labour.

Patriotism is the virtue of the vicious.

He hasn't a single redeeming vice.

VULGARITY

It is very vulgar to talk like a dentist
when one isn't a dentist.
It produces a false impression.

Modern journalism justifies its own
existence by the great Darwinian principle
of the survival of the vulgarest.

Vulgarity is simply the conduct
of other people, just as falsehoods
are the truth of other people.

WOMEN

I don't believe in women
who think too much.
Women should think in moderation, as
they should do all things in moderation.

No woman is a genius.
Women are a decorative sex.
They never have anything to say,
but they say it charmingly.

No woman should have a memory.
Memory in a woman is the beginning
of dowdiness.

Plain women are always jealous of their
husbands, beautiful women never are;
they have no time, they are always
occupied in being jealous of
other people's husbands.

WORK

An individual who has to make things for the use of others, and with reference to their wants and their wishes, does not work with interest, and consequently cannot put into his work what is best in him.

I am hard at work being idle.

Industry is the root of all ugliness.

LADY BRACKNELL: ...Do you smoke?
JACK: Well, yes, I must admit I smoke.
LADY BRACKNELL: I am glad to hear it. A man should always have an occupation of some kind. There are far too many idle men in London as it is.

Last Words

Referring to his bedroom curtains:
Either they go,
or I do.